EDGE BOOKS™

WARRIORS OF HISTORY

VIKINGS

by Allison Lassieur

Consultant:
Dr. Roland Thorstensson
Professor of Scandinavian Studies
Gustavus Adolphus College
St. Peter, Minnesota

Capstone
press

Mankato, Minnesota

Edge Books are published by Capstone Press,
151 Good Counsel Drive, P.O. Box 669, Mankato, Minnesota 56002.
www.capstonepress.com

Library of Congress Cataloging-in-Publication Data
Lassieur, Allison.
    The Vikings / by Allison Lassieur.
    p. cm.—(Edge Books. Warriors of History)
    ISBN-13: 978-0-7368-6434-3 (hardcover)
    ISBN-10: 0-7368-6434-2 (hardcover)
1. Vikings—Warfare—Juvenile literature. I. Title. II. Series.
DL65.L376 2007
948'022—dc22   2005034931

Summary: Describes the Vikings, including their history, weapons, and way of life.

Editorial Credits
Mandy Robbins, editor; Thomas Emery, designer; Cynthia Martin, illustrator;
    Kim Brown, production artist; Jo Miller, photo researcher; Scott Thoms,
    photo editor

Photo Credits
The Árni Magnússon Institute in Iceland, 14
Art Directors/David Mcgill, cover
Art Resource, NY/Werner Forman, 22
Corbis/Bettmann, 8–9, 28–29; Christopher Cormack, 4; Nik Wheeler, 25
Getty Images Inc./Hulton Archive, 27; Spencer Arnold, 16–17
The Granger Collection, New York, 6, 18, 24
Mary Evans Picture Library/Douglas McCarthy, 10
North Wind Picture Archives, 12

1 2 3 4 5 6 11 10 09 08 07 06

TABLE OF CONTENTS

CHAPTER 1

THE WORLD OF THE VIKINGS

LEARN ABOUT:
- The first raid
- Viking society
- Why Vikings raided

Today, crumbling rocks are all that remain of the Lindisfarne monastery.

The date was June 8, 793. It was a lovely summer day at the Lindisfarne monastery in Ireland. The monastery was built on a lonely bit of land overlooking the sea. The monks who lived there went about their business that day. Suddenly, one of them saw several long ships on the horizon.

At first, the monks were happy. Finally, someone had sent supplies to their small church. But their happiness soon turned to terror. These were not supply ships.

When the ships landed, fierce men jumped out, waving weapons. With a battle cry, the invaders attacked. They killed many of the monks and took the rest captive. The raiders stole gold plates, silver goblets, jeweled book covers, and candlesticks. When all was destroyed, these mysterious men climbed aboard their ships and sailed away.

Viking warriors took many of the monks from Lindisfarne as slaves.

The attack on the peaceful monastery shocked the people of Europe. Most Europeans were Christians. From their point of view, attacking a Christian monastery was a horrible act.

But the men who had attacked the monastery were not Christians. They worshipped other gods. For years, these Northmen, or Norse, raided churches and towns along European coasts. No one was safe.

A BRUTAL ATTACK

Several descriptions of the raid on the Lindisfarne monastery exist today. The *Anglo-Saxon Chronicles*, written during the time of the Vikings, reports:

"And they came to the church of Lindisfarne, laid everything waste with grievous plundering, trampled the holy places with polluted steps, dug up the altars and seized all the treasures of the holy church. They killed some of the brothers, took some away with them in fetters, many they drove out, naked and loaded with insults, some they drowned in the sea . . ."

WARRIORS OF THE NORTH

Most Europeans thought the Northmen were heartless men who lived on the seas, searching for victims. But there was more to the Norse warriors, or Vikings. They lived north of Europe and east of England in an area called Scandinavia.

Vikings traveled in boats called longships. These ships could be rowed right up on shore.

Scandinavia is a large area that includes the present-day countries of Denmark, Sweden, and Norway. Most Vikings were farmers. The richest Vikings owned the most land. The wealthiest land owners became leaders called jarls. Jarls fought one another for more land and power.

Seeing a group of ferocious Vikings climb ashore would strike fear in the heart of any European.

Vikings loyal to a leader would fight for him. Jarls rewarded their warriors with land and riches. But over time, land in Scandinavia became scarce. Vikings who wanted wealth had to find it somewhere else. They raided monasteries and towns all over Europe. Vikings soon became the most famous and feared warriors in the world.

EDGE FACT

In the early 900s, a fierce Viking called Rollo the Great conquered much of present-day France.

CHAPTER II
DISHONOR IS WORSE THAN DEATH

LEARN ABOUT:

- *The fighting season*
- *Dishonor*
- *Revenge*

Bravery was one of the most valued character traits in Viking culture.

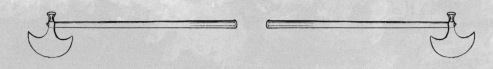

The Vikings did not have an army. Most men were farmers, merchants, or traders. But when battles began, every man became a warrior.

Summer was the time for fighting. During this season, some Viking clans, or family groups, fought for land in Scandinavia.

Other Vikings boarded longships in search of treasure beyond their homelands. These Vikings were the raiders who attacked and plundered Europe.

When summer was over, Vikings returned home. They put away their weapons, harvested crops, and settled in for the long winter.

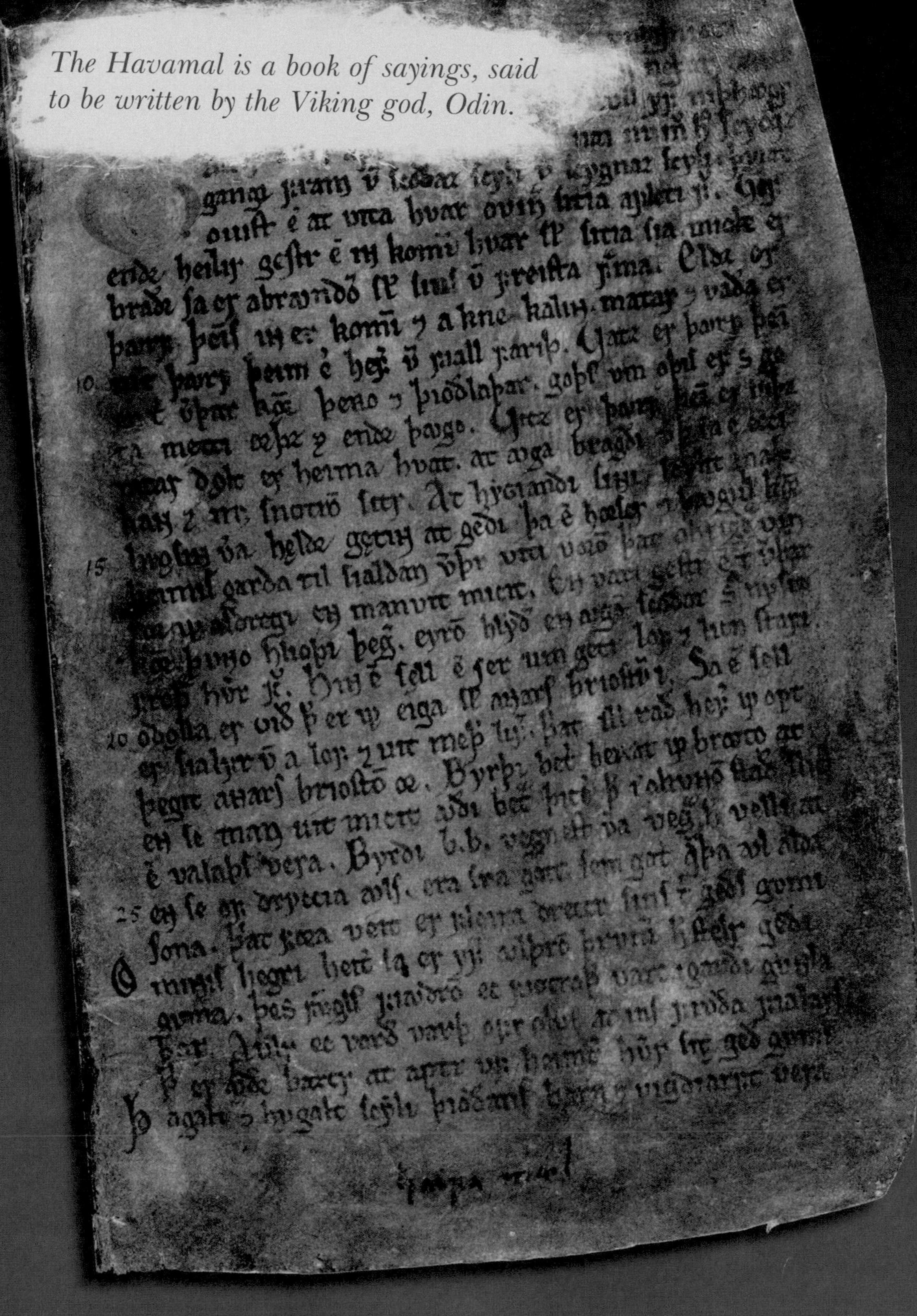

The Havamal is a book of sayings, said to be written by the Viking god, Odin.

HONOR IS EVERYTHING

Honor, trust, and wisdom are not words that many people would use to describe Vikings. But Viking warriors lived by a strong code of honor.

Vikings accepted the fact that all people die. Honor was what really mattered. A skilled warrior who had killed many enemies was held in high honor. But strength in battles wasn't enough. An honorable Viking was loyal to his friends and cared for his family. He acted with wisdom and fairness.

To a Viking warrior, the opposite of honor was disgrace. Committing a crime was considered disgraceful. So was being fooled by a rival in war or business. Disgrace could bring shamc to a family for generations. To a Viking, dishonoring one's family was worse than death.

EDGE FACT

One of the sayings in the Havamal is, "Cattle die, and kinsmen die, but honor never dies."

REVENGE

If a Viking warrior was disgraced, he had to restore his honor. Revenge was the only way to do this. A Viking who didn't seek revenge against an enemy was considered weak.

A Viking could also seek revenge for a disgrace that was not his own. It was a warrior's duty to help family members and friends gain revenge. Most Vikings could call an army of loyal warriors to their side. Together, they would attack the man or clan who had caused the disgrace.

Many of the bloody battles between Viking clans were for revenge.

CHAPTER III

WEAPONS OF THE VIKINGS

LEARN ABOUT:

- *Favorite weapon*
- *Spears and axes*
- *Armor*

Viking swords were made extremely strong using layers of steel and iron.

A Viking's weapons were his most valuable possessions. A poor Viking might only have an axe or a spear. A wealthy warrior would usually own a sword, shield, and armor. Vikings rarely left home without their weapons. Viking farmers tilled the fields with their weapons at their sides. Vikings even slept with their weapons beside them.

SWORDS

A Viking sword had a thin, double-edged blade that was nearly 3 feet (1 meter) long. Handles, called hilts, were made of bone, ivory, or metal. Hilts were decorated with gold, silver, and jewels.

A sword was a prized weapon. Sometimes warriors gave swords to one another as gifts. Swords were also passed down from father to son. Vikings wrote poetry about their swords. Many Vikings were even buried with them.

Helmet
Viking helmets did not have horns, though they are often shown that way.

Chain mail
Warriors who wore chain mail had to wear thick padding underneath so that the metal rings didn't cut their skin.

Spear
Spears were the most common Viking weapons.

Shield
The first Viking shields were circular. Later, shields were shaped like kites to protect the legs.

SPEARS AND AXES

Viking warriors also used spears and axes in battle. Most spear blades were 18 inches (46 centimeters) long. Battle axes had a large handle and a thin blade. Sometimes a Viking attacked with an axe in one hand and a sword in the other.

ARMOR

Viking warriors did not wear much armor. The average warrior owned an iron helmet. Very rich warriors could afford a chain mail shirt. Chain mail, made of interlocking metal rings, was good protection against enemy weapons. Poorer Vikings had to make do with leather armor.

Many Viking warriors carried wooden shields to protect themselves in battle. A Viking shield was flat and round, with a hand grip in the middle. The shields were big enough to cover a warrior from his chin to his knees.

CHAPTER IV
A PROUD CULTURE FADES AWAY

LEARN ABOUT:
- The Great Army
- Finding new homes
- The last great battle

Beautifully carved Viking helmets have been found in grave sites all over Europe.

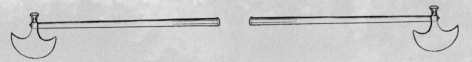

For more than 40 years, Viking warriors attacked the coasts of England, Ireland, and Scotland. In the mid-800s, a huge Viking army called the Great Army arrived in England. They were looking for new lands to settle. The Great Army cut a path through England, killing and raiding as they went.

Finally, King Alfred the Great of England made a deal with the Vikings. If they stopped fighting, he would give them the northern half of England. The Vikings agreed. Their new homeland was called the Danelaw.

Groups of Vikings also settled in other countries. Viking raiders attacked and settled in parts of what is now France, Ireland, and Russia. The Vikings, who had once traveled the high seas, began to settle down.

A Viking called Erik the Red led 25 shiploads of people to Greenland in 986.

EXPLORING NEW LANDS

Some Vikings weren't content to settle in Europe. They wanted more adventure. Large groups of Vikings sailed west. They settled in Iceland, and later, Greenland. Some Vikings sailed even farther west. These Vikings reached North America around the year 1000, nearly 500 years before Christopher Columbus.

*Erik the Red's son, Leif Eriksson,
became the first European to set foot
on North American soil.*

END OF THE VIKING ERA

After settling in other lands, Vikings married local people. Their children learned local languages and customs. Many Vikings became Christians. They left their old ways behind.

In Scandinavia, kings such as Harald Fairhair rose to power. Local jarls no longer had control. Fighting among clans stopped. By the late 1000s, most of the Viking culture had faded away.

LAST VIKING BATTLES

In 1035, England's King Edward died. The king had wanted a Viking named Harald Godwinsson to take his place. But two other men of Viking heritage wanted the position. One was King Harald Sigurdsson of Norway. The other was William of Normandy. William was from France, but one of his ancestors was the famous Viking, Rollo the Great.

Statues in Norway honor King Harald Fairhair, who is responsible for uniting the country.

EDGE FACT

Legend has it that King Harald Fairhair didn't cut his hair until he had united all of Norway.

In the fall of 1066, Godwinsson's army attacked Sigurdsson's forces in England. The battle was fierce and bloody. Finally, Sigurdsson was killed in battle. Godwinsson had won.

But a worse battle was coming. William of Normandy had sailed to England with an army of his own. When Godwinsson found out, he rushed to a place called Hastings in southern England.

A FAMOUS BATTLE

The Battle of Hastings is one of the most famous battles in history. It began the morning of October 14, 1066, and lasted all day.

More than 5,000 warriors met their deaths during the Battle of Hastings.

Godwinsson's army was winning, until he was killed in battle. At the end of the day, William of Normandy had won. On December 25, 1066, he was crowned King of England.

After William's victory, the Vikings' world changed. Those who had settled in England came under control of William's new government. In the north, Scandinavia had broken into the countries of Denmark, Norway, and Sweden. These new kingdoms were more concerned with local business than sailing to other lands. After nearly 300 years, the days of Viking adventurers were over.

GLOSSARY

clan (KLAN)—a large group of related families

culture (KUHL-chur)—a people's way of life, ideas, art, customs, and traditions

jarl (YARL)—a Viking leader

monastery (MAH-nuh-ster-ee)—a group of buildings where monks live and work

raid (RAYD)—a sudden, surprise attack on a place

revenge (ri-VENJ)—action taken in return for an injury or offense

heritage (HER-uh-tij)—property or traditions that are handed down from ancestors

plunder (PLUHN-dur)—to steal things by force, often during battle

READ MORE

Berger, Melvin, and Gilda Berger. *The Real Vikings: Craftsmen, Traders, and Fearsome Raiders.* Washington, D.C.: National Geographic, 2003.

Margeson, Susan M. *Viking.* DK Eyewitness Books. New York: DK, 2005.

INTERNET SITES

FactHound offers a safe, fun way to find Internet sites related to this book. All of the sites on FactHound have been researched by our staff.

Here's how:

1. Visit *www.facthound.com*

2. Choose your grade level.

3. Type in this book ID **0736864342** for age-appropriate sites. You may also browse subjects by clicking on letters, or by clicking on pictures and words.

4. Click on the **Fetch It** button.

FactHound will fetch the best sites for you!

INDEX